Loving tne Lost

By
Rebecca Perone Kostrzewski

ISBN: 979-8-89525-430-1

Prologue

She wore her pain like a dress, stitched with dignity and adorned with stories that brightened her days. A passion that originated from deep within her soul, Rebecca clung to her writings, creating Loving the Lost as her own book of feelings throughout the grieving process. Giving you Loving the Lost, the best of her poems written to date, she never gave up, no matter how hard the situation may be, she kept her head held mostly high, her spirit unbreakable.

Dedication

I would like to dedicate this book to my mother, Francesca, I love you.

November 5 1947-January 4 2022

Acknowledgement

I want to take a minute to express my heartfelt gratitude to my family, who have been my rock through thick and thin. Their unwavering support and unconditional love have been a constant source of strength for me, and I am forever in their debt.

I would also like to thank everyone from the crowds that have been cheering me on through this journey, never letting me give up, and helping me keep pushing forward. Thank you for your dedication.

Contents

Work and Life

Working every day

Just to keep a way

To balance money and life

Sometimes sharper than a knife

Everything you love is growing

And you go on knowing

That you are missing everything

Like the very breath you are breathing

You start to see they are cheating

This very life you're living

As your children grow without you

It's enough to make you stew

Why does retirement happen

When everything you worked to manage

Grows away from you?

Without my Person

After losing your person

You learn a valuable lesson

The lesson of what being alone truly means

The world around you no longer what it seems

All the faces might stay the same

But in the end, it's the same game

You start to shut out everyone

You find no amusement, not even in the sun

The emptiness keeps growing

Like a tumour on the groin

You look for comfort in familiarity

Maybe someone can help give you clarity

Of why all the bad things happen to you

You may feel alone this is true....

New possibilities gone so fast

Nothing seems to last

No matter the situation,

You'll have the same Revelation

Nothing will ever replace your person

Not even a single version

Come sit with me now,

We can be alone.Together

Long lost love

Missing you is something I do

It's honestly nothing new

I now hold you tightly

In my heart nightly

I dream of you daily,

It drives me crazy

Not to be with you

This much is true

My friend you shall be

Until I am set free

So please stay patient with me

And you will see

Our lives will be better

And everything that can matter

Will fall in perfect place

When we win this race

Lost and lonely

Lost and lonely
This you've done to me
Strolling this corridor
Nothing I can ignore
My head no longer hurts
From all of your nasty words
Something that used to bug me
Now just makes me free.
Like a butterfly
Passing you by
I hear you make a sigh
Wishing to surely die
Lost and lonely
No longer to be seen
Hurting no more
I won the final score

Music and Melody

Connecting to the world

Using tunes and words

Understanding stories riddled

By untold nerves

An artist laughed with emotions

A hurt behind the eyes

Behind this devotion

Clear for the skies

To hear the sound

Of a broken heart

Rumbling the Earth's shattered ground

As fast as a dart

Their souls passed by

In the words they plastered

In truth they lye

Memories

Going so fast

A moment gone too soon

Making a memory last

Like a melody or a tune

Stuck in your head

Even after bed

Memories can turn dark

Like an evening mark.

Remembering the good times

And all the nursery rhymes

And those who helped

Feelings that you felt.

The memories might surely fade

Voices that once made

You feel comfortable

Now make you feel sorrow

But the memories remain

A constant reminder

I what once was......

Death Prevails

Walking slowly

Across the corridor

I realize

Everything you've done for me.

Now I'm kneeling to the floor

Praying for him to do more

Not believing this is it

Now feeling this final hit

Prayers and wishes failed

But you'll still prevail

Across my memory

For others to see

You've become me

Cupid

Cupid once saw me

Crying under a tree

Not sure what was plaguing

The girl he could see

Hesitating

"Little lady please

Tears shine so deeply

Let me help the pain seize"

He said to me sheepishly

Listening I obliged

As he turned away

A pinch I felt

Like the sting of a belt

Across my heart

This is your art

Now he stands before me

This man I can now see

Telling me he loves me

Unconditionally

Finding the Light

They tell me there is a light

At the end of the tunnel so bright

That it will captivate your soul

I hope one day to know

If what they say is true

I feel like I've been running

For so long now I'm shaking

From a past so frightening

It's almost daunting

For the story I'd have to say

To still be here, to find a way

TO be standing here today

Maybe that light is near

And there will be no more fear

Different

Here I sit again

Head in my hands again

Wondering when this all ends

The truth that mends

The wounds I hold so deep

Looking like wildflowers as I sleep

Drifting so deeply in the scent

Knowing why I'm so bent

Wishing things were different

The way they were meant

But this is the path I'm on

Someday to be a swan

Burning Bridges

Misery loves company
As this I know is true
As I've been sitting here
Out here watching you
Burning the bridges
So tenderly you built
With all of the relationships
You never truly felt
Now you're left alone
In a world you once loved
Wondering why
Nothing can get solved
Strangers try to befriend you
But it's nothing new
Something always happening
Helping you to stew

Friends

Remembering all the fun we've had

Can sometimes make me sad

Missing you is something i now do

Because life is not fun without you

My friend you've been for so long

I replay your memories just like a song

To hold your hand again

Would be God sent

Like that of a bottle of champagne

Smooth and comforting

My heart is now fluttering

As I remember you

And everything I once knew

My heart

My hearts been broken

Time and time again

Now I'm left wide open

Looking at you, my friend

You've been there for me

Though thick and thin

Even when I thought that I'd

Never see you again.

We started out life's journey

As friends till the end.

But now you're more than that

The person you once were

You've become so much more

The man that I adore.

My hearts left on this table

For you to have and to hold

Just please keep it stable

Until we get old.

Depressed love

Here I see you looking at me

I wonder what it is you see

That's got you so intrigued

I wish everything you dreamed

Was everything that it seems

But the truth of the matter is

I am so depressed behind everything

I am afraid there is no reaching

The very depths of me

If only you knew the life I once had

You would understand

Why I feel this way now

I used to have everything you could imagine

I had my entire family

Without even realizing it

We were mostly happy

But we lost it all

Surrender

Nothing can prepare you

For the inevitable end.

The one meant for you

The answers for you to mend

They will not come with ease

This awful disease

So surrender yourself

The betterment of your health

From running unstable

To avoiding another label

This you have done to me

Little can you see

The tears flowing slowly

Forming streams unsteadily

Moistening my face

Leaving a funny taste

So now I must surrender

No longer a prisoner

So set me free

Alone

By Rebecca Perone Kostrzewski

Sitting alone again

Something I've grown used to

Alone in my head

With nowhere else to go

What is the truth

I ask so often

As my body is constantly giving out on me.

Why am I here?

To be tournamented by all your hateful words?

No one really cares about me

If they did, I wouldn't be

Alone

Love the Lonely

Love the lonely

They are the only

Ones that know

The highs and low

Of a broken heart

The last thing that sets them apart

IS they only want to fill the void

In their heart that been soiled

By everyone who held it

Before you lit

The flame in the voided part

Of their once broken heart

Drowning

Someday I will wander

To the ocean to ponder

On all the things I've witnessed

I have made this commitment

There is no turning back now

Maybe, though, just somehow

The water will be soothing

As it starts rushing in, moving

I am becoming one with the current

Now I'm begging for a god send

Blessings from above

Like that of a dove

Fear evokes me as the darkness

Comes and hugs me like a harness

I'm breathing less now

Maybe somehow

The waters devouring me

To be part of the deep blue sea

Never to ponder again

The waters my only friend.

I'm here

Driving in the car

You're my shining star

Chauffeuring me around town

As the wheels spin around

To work I go

Another show

Until I can

See you again

My beautiful friend

Now I await for you to get me

I see you waiting under that tree.

Bring me home so I can see

All that you mean to me

Please always remember what you see

I'm never leaving

My beautiful friend

Motherless daughter

Whispers in the wind

Remind me of the words you said

The comfort of my blankets

For all the hugs we held

The tears I shed

Remind me of the pains you felt

The day you lost your mother

And I held your hand

Now I'm the motherless daughter

Struggling to get through

Everything constantly reminds me of you

The way you laughed

To light up a room

To the way you cooked

Filled the table for an army

Even if cooking for two

God knows how much I miss you

And everything you stood for

Someday I will be with you again

Breaking Free

You've put me on the sidelines

The place you've needed me most

Now I'm left wondering

My shadow left to shine

My ghost is your host

Instilling in my fear

I've been left unbroken

To sit on a shelf

A toy you now claim a token

You say it's for my health

No longer will I stay here

In the place you hold dear

Myself with the angels and demons

Sitting alone in the dark

I hear an evil snark

Wailing sharply

Making me hardly

Hear anything at all

Is this in my head

All that's been said

Or am I dreaming at all?

The noise grows faint

Now before me a saint

He knelt before me and washed my feet

Before he took that lovely seat

Sitting before me, The noise now will whisper

So soft, I thought, it'd disappear

The same turned and looked at me and said

"Young child don't be scared

Your father is up there and he still cared

For all the sins he gave his son

Now let's give hell a good run

With that the noise grew again

And I knew I needed to mend

Casting demons out with all my might

The Angel thought it was a beautiful sight

A New Chapter

Remembering the past to regain your future

Let it hit you like Gods rapture

He's flipping pages, creating a new chapter

Knowing someday it will be better

He sees your pain and suffering

So now he's here with an offering

May the blessings he gives you

Be enough that you view

Everything with open eyes

May you know this is not a guise

This is simply your prize

For continuing your journey

Even though you weren't sturdy

Remember you are worthy

To receive God's mercy

Forgotten

Am I the forgotten

This I have to ask

As the world spins past me

Going way too fast

Am I the forgotten

That's come in at last?

Head held low

For this evening mass

Am I the forgotten

The one you have replaced

With a new body, new hair and new face

Am I the forgotten

A feather within the wind

Blowing past, you

To never be seen again

A letter to Mom

I wish so bad to call you

Just so I can tell you

Everything happening now

It's enough to make you drown

To hear your words of wisdom

Is something I need, I miss them

God took you too soon this is true

But I know he needed you too

Sometimes I sit and wonder

(And it will fright me light that of thunder)

If things will get better

Like that of the weather

If you were still here today

What would you say

To make my fears go away

Surrender

Nothing can prepare you
For the inevitable end.
The one meant for you,
The answers for you to mend.
They will not come with ease,
This awful disease...
So surrender yourself,
The betterment of your health
From running unstable
To avoiding another label
This you have done to me
Little can you see
The tears flowing slowly
Forming streams unsteadily
Moistening my face
Leaving a funny taste
So now I must surrender
No longer a prisoner
So set me free

I Am Only a Lingering Thought

I am the forgotten

This much is true

Putting all my energy

In something great like you.

I am the forgotten

Stumbling and sore

From all the attention

I get no more.

I am the forgotten

So many things I've said

Now rest upon ears

Fastened to your head.

I am the forgotten

The wisdom I bestowed

Now settles upon you

Like a final blow.

I am the forgotten

The mask and the tears

The ones you used to dry

Upon so many years.

Will you remember all that I did

When the lights go out

And I am just a lingering thought.

Made in the USA
Columbia, SC
28 December 2024

48622435R00020